Destination

GERMANY

GW01463960

MARY SMITH

Headway · Hodder & Stoughton

Acknowledgements

With thanks to Joanna, Ian and Alison from Cedars Upper School, Linslade, who were partnered with students from the Kreisgymnasium Hochschwarzwald; special thanks to Klaus and Christoph, our friends in the Black Forest; also to Nicole Müller who checked all the language and to Pauline Wolfenden who checked the script.

The author and publisher would like to thank the following for permission to reproduce photographs: German National Tourist Office, p. 34; Robert Harding Picture Library, p. 53; Mill Graphics, p. 28; Roddy Paine, pp. 20, 22, 24, 38, 47, 55; Skishoot, p. 35; Zefa, pp. 1, 33, 40, 49.

British Library Cataloguing in Publication Data
Smith, Mary
   Destination Germany: a handbook for school visit.
   1. German language
   I. Title
   430

   ISBN 0 340 52802 8

First published 1990

© 1990 M. Smith   Illustration © Katinka Kew   Cover Illustration © Sue Dray

Typeset by Wearside Tradespools, Fulwell, Sunderland
Printed in Hong Kong for the educational publishing division of Hodder and Stoughton Ltd, Mill Road, Dunton Green, Sevenoaks, Kent by Wing King Tong

Contents

Contents

Introduction

If you are a young person and you are going to live with a German-speaking family, whether on a brief exchange visit or for a longer period, then *Destination Germany* is the book for you! It is designed to help you feel at home in your partner's family and is filled with the sentences you may need but might forget at the crucial moment.

This book covers not only the German phrases which you will find useful, but also contains hints on coping with the German or Austrian way of life, to make you feel more at ease in your new surroundings.

Once you get the hang of it, it won't be too difficult to ask questions in a foreign language, but it is not always easy to understand the answer! To help overcome this kind of problem, each chapter also contains sentences you might hear, such as instructions or information, together with the meaning in English.

Usually, we give straightforward sentences to help you. Where it is appropriate, we have given more complex sentences and in this case we have marked them with symbols:

- simple sentence, easy to remember;
▶ more complicated sentence with harder grammar.

If you have the cassette which accompanies this book, try listening to it with the book in front of you. This will help you to pronounce any unfamiliar words and to recognise the sounds when you hear them in use.

Destination Germany will fit easily into your pocket, so you can carry it with you throughout your stay. Let it help you to enjoy your visit to Austria, Germany or the German-speaking parts of Switzerland.

Don't Worry

Germany is a large country and people in various parts speak their own special dialects, such as Schwäbisch, Allemanisch or Bavarian. These are not just different accents, but have evolved from other languages, so that you will hear different words, too.

However, all children learn **Hochdeutsch** at school. This is the German which we learn in class in Britain. German newspapers, radio and television all use **Hochdeutsch**, which means that all the members of the family will know standard German, even if they don't usually use it in conversation together.

If you have difficulty in following what is being said, some of these queries may help:

Können Sie langsamer sprechen, bitte? *Could you speak slower, please?*

Kannst du langsamer sprechen, bitte? *Could you speak slower, please?* (friendly)

Langsam, bitte, ich verstehe nicht.   *Slower, please, I don't understand.*

Können Sie Hochdeutsch sprechen?   *Please could you speak standard German?*

Kannst du Hochdeutsch sprechen?   *Could you speak standard German?* (friendly)
Wie, bitte?   *Pardon?/What did you say?*

Friendly or Formal?

When you are talking to your partner you'll use the friendly **du** form of verbs and also **dich**, **dir**, **dein**. If you're with a group of friends, you'll need the plural friendly form, **ihr**, along with **euch** and **euer**. But you'll use the more formal **Sie**, **Ihnen**, **Ihr** to all the adults. Germans are more formal in their speech and even adults who know each other quite well use **Sie** together. In formal situations (when you're in a shop or at the doctor, for example), teenagers are addressed as **Sie**, too.

If you do get muddled, people will understand and not be insulted. Just smile and say:

Verzeihung!   *Excuse me.*

Entschuldigung!   *Excuse me.*

Tschuldigung!   *Excuse me.*

Someone is sure to help you if you get muddled again.

Meeting the Family

The Germans and Austrians are enthusiastic hand shakers when meeting and when leaving each other; you'll also find that there will be hand-shaking all round each time you meet people, not just when you're initially introduced.

Tag!...Tag!...Tag! Au! Meine Hand!

Things you may hear as you are welcomed:

Guten Tag. *Good day/hello.*

Guten Abend. *Good evening.*

Grüß Gott. *Hello* (used in Austria and S. Germany).

Willkommen bei uns. *Welcome to our family.*

Wie geht es dir? *How are you?*

Wie geht's? *How's things/How's it going?*

Don't be surprised to be greeted by **"Hallo!"** as well. At first just used on the telephone, it is now often used by young people when they meet each other.

You don't need to reply in long sentences!

Guten Tag. *Hello.*

Angenehm. *Pleased to meet you.*

Es geht mir gut, danke. *I'm very well, thank you.*

Und Ihnen?/Und dir? *How are you?*

Sehr erfreut. *Glad to know you.*

The journey

The family will probably enquire about your journey:

Wie war deine Reise?   *How was your journey?*

Die Reise, war sie gut?   *Was your journey good?*

War deine Reise gut?   *Was your journey good?*

Hast du eine gute Reise gehabt?   *Did you have a good journey?*

Here are some replies for you to choose from:

Es war eine gute Reise.   *It was a good journey.*

Die Reise war schlecht!   *The journey was awful!*

Sie war nicht so gut.   *It was not too good.*

Sie war nicht so schlecht.   *It was not too bad.*

Ich war seekrank und ich bin noch krank.   *I was seasick and I'm still poorly.*

Ich war seekrank, aber mir geht es jetzt besser.   *I was seasick but I'm better now.*

How do you feel?

You will probably be asked:

Bist du müde?   *Are you tired?*

Hast du Hunger?   *Are you hungry?*

Hast du Durst?   *Are you thirsty?*

Willst du schlafen?   *Would you like a sleep?*

Here are some of the answers you may need:

Ja, gerne.   *Oh yes, please.*

Nein, danke.   *No thanks.*

Ich will/Ich möchte etwas essen/trinken.   *I want/I'd like something to eat/drink.*

Ich bin sehr hungrig/durstig.   *I'm very hungry/thirsty.*

Ich habe großen Hunger/Durst.   *I'm ever so hungry/thirsty.*

Ich habe keinen Hunger/Durst.   *I'm not hungry/thirsty.*

Ich bin zu müde.   *I'm too tired.*

If a meal has been prepared but you really are too tired to eat, or feel sick with exhaustion, you may wish to refuse food, but without upsetting anybody:

● **Ich bin sehr müde. Vielleicht darf ich später essen?**   *I'm very tired. Perhaps I could eat later?*

▶ **Entschuldigung, ich bin sehr müde, und kann im Moment nichts essen.**   *Sorry, I'm very tired and couldn't eat anything at the moment.*

Giving a gift

It is a nice idea to give your host family a small gift on your arrival. You might pack a present in your hand luggage to give soon after you arrive. Something typically British or a regional speciality would be ideal, but nothing too fragile nor too heavy!

And as you hand over your gift:

Hier ist ein Geschenk aus England für Sie/dich.   *Here is a present from England for you.*

Meine Eltern danken Ihnen, und hier ist ihr Geschenk.   *My parents send their thanks, here is their present.*

Aber es war echt Wedgwood!

Settling In

First necessity!

Asking for the toilet or bathroom is not difficult:

Wo ist die Toilette, bitte?   *Where's the toilet, please.*

Wo ist das Badezimmer, bitte?   *Where's the bathroom, please?*

Wo ist das Klo, bitte?   *Where's the loo, please?*

> The mechanics of German and Austrian plumbing are
> frequently different from what we are used to here in Britain.
> You may find a variety of flushing mechanisms which you
> haven't come across before. If there is no handle or chain, look
> for a button or lever which, on some modern toilets, may be
> disguised as part of the cistern.

Public Conveniences

Public toilets are often free, but if you have to pay, you will need to
have a selection of small coins with you.

If you don't have the correct coins, you'll need to ask someone:

Haben Sie Kleingeld, bitte?   *Have you got some small change,
please?*

You may find that even the
gentlemen's toilets need coins,
although most are free.
Sometimes an attendant will take
the money from you, then clean
the toilet before you enter. And
you'll often find a woman in
charge of the gentlemen's toilet!

If you need to use the toilet but cannot find a public one, you will
be relieved to know that all restaurants and cafés have to provide
these facilities by law – so comfort can be restored for the price of a
drink! In modern restaurants, at motorway service areas, etc, a new
type of washbasin is found – with no tap! An electronic eye senses

when you put your hands into the basin and then the water is issued automatically.

If you cannot understand the instructions you find, or there are none, wait and discreetly watch other people!

These questions will help if you do need to ask how things work:

Wie funktioniert das?   *How does this work?*

Wie funktioniert das Stöpsel?   *How does the plug work?*

Wie funktioniert der Wasserhahn?   *How does the tap work?*

Your room

Whatever the state of your room at home, try to keep your belongings tidy when you are a visitor!

If you are not sure where to put things, ask:

Wohin soll ich ... legen?   *Where shall I put ... ?*

Wo soll ich ... hinlegen?   *Where shall I put ... ?*
   ... meinen Koffer ...   *... my suitcase?*
   ... mein Badetuch ...   *... my bath towel?*
   ... mein Handtuch ...   *... my hand towel?*
   ... meine Sachen ...   *... my things?*
   ... meine Kleider ...   *... my clothes?*

If you need an extra blanket, towel or pillow, say:

Ich brauche noch eine Decke/ein Handtuch/ein Kissen (ein Polster – Austria)

Electrical equipment

If you have brought electrical equipment with you, you'll need to check that the plug is suitable for use in the continental socket.

Funktioniert dieser Stecker hier?   *Will this plug work here?*

German and Austrian sockets are two-pin with round holes and the holes are spaced slightly closer together than in a British razor point. An adaptor plug can be bought in Britain before you leave. Large stores, chemists and electrical shops stock these at a reasonable price.

The German round two-pin plugs are called **Schukostecker**. If your equipment will not work you can explain:

Ich habe keinen Schukostecker.   *I haven't got a continental plug.*

Ich habe keinen deutschen Stecker.   *I haven't got a German plug.*

Then you can ask for what you need:

● Ich brauche einen Fön/einen Rasierapparat.   *I need a hairdryer/razor.*

▶ Können Sie/Kannst du mir bitte einen Fön/einen Rasierapparat geben?   *Could you please lend me a hairdryer/razor?*

The sockets are not found down by the skirting board, but conveniently at waist height. Razor points in bathrooms are sometimes covered by a little safety flap because they may be next to the washbasin. People also plug their hairdryers in this socket, as it is not illegal to use electrical equipment in the bathroom although it is in Britain.

Es ist keine Steckdose da!

Aber sie ist hier!

Washing and ironing

During your stay some of your clothes may need to be washed or ironed. This is not normally a problem as the mother usually offers to do it when she does her family wash. She may say to you something like this:

Ich wasche heute, hast du etwas für die Waschmachine?   *I'm going to do the washing today, have you anything to go in the machine?*

If there is a laundry basket, she'll show you where it is:

Lege deine Wäsche hinein.   *Put your washing in here.*

However, if nobody mentions it, you may need to ask:

Würden Sie das bitte für mich waschen?   *Would you wash that for me, please?*

Ich muß etwas waschen. Haben Sie Waschpulver, bitte?   *I have to do some washing. Do you have any washing powder, please?*

Luckily the washmark symbols on clothing labels are internationally recognised, so you won't need to explain how to care for anything delicate.

If your clothes are badly creased from the journey, or if you'd like to iron something before you go out, you could ask:

Darf ich das bitte bügeln?   *May I iron that please?*

Würden Sie das bitte für mich bügeln?   *Please would you iron that for me?*

Anything you need

If you should run out of anything essential or forget something you needed, use the following to make the sentences you need.

Ich brauche . . .   *I need . . .*

Ich habe . . . vergessen.   *I've forgotten . . .*

Ich habe . . . verloren.   *I've lost . . .*

Ich möchte . . . kaufen.   *I'd like to buy . . .*

Können Sie mir bitte . . . geben?   *Could you please give me . . . ?*

Darf ich bitte Ihr/Ihren . . . borgen?   *May I borrow your . . . ?*
   . . . ein/mein Handtuch . . .   . . . *hand towel*
   . . . ein/mein Badetuch . . .   . . . *bath towel*
   . . . ein/mein Deodorans . . .   . . . *deodorant*
   . . . ein/mein Shampoo . . .   . . . *shampoo*

... eine/meine Spülung ...   ... conditioner
... eine/meine Zahnpaste ...   ... toothpaste
... eine/meine Zahnbürste ...   toothbrush
... eine/meine Haarbürste ...   ... hairbrush
... eine/meine Duschlotion ...   ... shower gel
... einen/meinen Puder ...   ... talc
... einen/meinen Kamm ...   ... comb
... einen/meinen Rasierapparat ...   ... razor

Other things you may need are:

... Seife ...   ... soap

... Aspirin ...   ... aspirin

... Halspastillen ...   ... throat pastilles

... Hustenbonbons ...   ... cough sweets

... Reisetabletten ...   ... travel tablets

... Tampons ...   ... tampons

... Binden/Monatsbinden ...   ... sanitary towels

If you have to replace your shampoo or conditioner, you'll need to look out for these words:

... für tägliche Haarwäsche ...   ... for everyday use.

... für trockenes Haar ...   ... for dry hair.

... für normales und kraftiges Haar ...   ... for normal and thick hair.

... für fettendes und feines Haar ...   ... for greasy and fine hair.

... für sprödes Haar ...   ... for brittle hair.

If you've run out of something, use this list:

Es ist . . . mehr da.   *There's no more . . . there.*

Es gibt . . . mehr.   *There isn't any more . . .*
   . . . **kein Tuch** . . .   . . . *towel*
   . . . **kein Toilettenpapier** . . .   . . . *toilet paper*
   . . . **kein Klopapier** . . .   . . . *loo roll*
   . . . **keine Seife** . . .   *soap*
   . . . **keine Kleiderbügel** . . .   *clothes hangers*

And if something is broken or out of order:

Es ist kaputt! (said in Germany)   **Es ist hin! (said in Austria)**

Bedtime

Normally Germans and Austrians don't eat late in the evening, and they don't often have supper. If you are used to a late snack at home you might want to bring something with you for when you feel peckish. Biscuits or wrapped health food bars are ideal, but not anything that might melt!

If you should be hungry or thirsty in the evening you could say:

Ich habe ein bißchen Hunger/Durst.   *I'm a little bit hungry/thirsty.*

Ich möchte etwas essen/trinken.   *I'd like something to eat/drink.*

> Should a **Betthupfer** be offered to you, that's a bedtime snack or a midnight feast.

If your host family seem tired, try not to stay up too late and if you feel worn out, don't feel you have to stay up longer than you normally do. You'll find it exhausting at first, especially when you are hearing German spoken all the time. Remember, too, that the time difference between the two countries will mean that you'll feel more tired until you get accustomed to it. If you feel ready for bed:

Ich möchte früh ins Bett gehen.   *I'd like to go to bed early.*

At bedtime the family may say some of these:

Gute Nacht!   *Good night!*

Schlaf' gut!   *Sleep well!*

Bis morgen.   *See you tomorrow.*

Bis morgen früh.   *Until tomorrow morning.* (This literally means 'the early part of tomorrow', i.e. before noon, not early in the morning!)

They said, "Bis morgen früh" I hope this is early enough.

Your reply could be:

Danke und gute Nacht.   *Thank you, good night.*

The next morning you'll probably be asked:

Hast du gut geschlafen?   *Did you have a good sleep?*

Bist du ausgeschlafen?   *Did you sleep well?*

And we hope that you'll be able to reply:

- **Ja danke, sehr gut.**   *Yes, thanks, very good.*
- **Ja, danke, ich habe gut geschlafen.**   *Yes, thanks, I did sleep well.*

Fitting In

Your host family will try to make you feel at home. They may even invite you to:

Fühl' dich wie zu Hause!   *Make yourself at home.*

But no thoughtful guest would behave exactly as at home!

As a visitor, try not to disrupt the life of your hosts too much. The hints below will help you feel more at ease with the family, and they will appreciate your consideration.

When is it convenient?

Enquire about the family routine so that you do not feel in the way, especially in the bathroom in the mornings!

Ways of asking when to get up:

- **Wann soll ich morgen aufstehen?**   *When should I get up tomorrow?*

- **Wann soll ich morgen früh aufstehen?**   *When should I get up tomorrow morning?*

▶ **Um wieviel Uhr stehe ich auf?**   *What time do I get up?*

▶ **Um wieviel Uhr soll ich aufstehen?**   *What time should I get up?*

Ways of asking if the bathroom is free:

- **Ist das Badezimmer frei?**   *Is the bathroom vacant?*

- **Ist die Dusche frei?**   *Is the shower free?*

▶ **Um wieviel Uhr ist das Badezimmer frei?**   *What time is the bathroom available?*

Ways of asking when breakfast will be ready:

- **Wann frühstücken wir?** *When do we breakfast?*
- **Wann gibt es Frühstück?** *When do we have breakfast?*
- ▶ **Um wieviel Uhr frühstücken wir?** *What time do we have breakfast?*
- ▶ **Um wieviel Uhr gibt es Frühstück?** *What time's breakfast?*

If you are going out and need to know when to be ready:

Wann muß ich fertig sein? *When must I be ready?*

Wann/Um wieviel Uhr fahren wir ab? *What time are we leaving?*

Or if you're going out without your partner and need to know when to be back:

Wann muß ich zurückkommen? *When must I be back?*

Asking permission

You can make the sentences you need from the phrases below:

Ich möchte ... *I'd like to ...*   **Darf ich ...** *May I ...*

Ich möchte gern ... *I'd very much like to ...*

Soll ich ...
- ... **Briefmarken kaufen.**
- ... **einen Brief schicken.**
- ... **meinen Freund/meine Freundin besuchen.**
- ... **zu Fuß gehen.**
- ... **meinen Freund/meine Freundin anrufen.**
- ... **meinem Freund/meiner Freundin telefonieren.**
- ... **meine Eltern anrufen.**
- ... **meinen Eltern telefonieren.**

Should I ...
- *... buy some stamps.*
- *... post a letter.*
- *... visit my friend.*
- *... go out on foot/walk there.*
- *... ring my friend.*
- *... 'phone my friend.*
- *... ring my parents.*
- *... 'phone my parents.*

Fitting In

It would be polite to offer to pay for any telephone calls, although the family may not want to take any money, especially for the local calls.

- **Wieviel kostet der Anruf?** *How much was the call?*
▶ **Was bekommen Sie für den Anruf?** *What do I owe you for the call?*

Phoning

Phoning in Germany and Austria is as easy as it is at home, but the dialling, ringing etc. sounds are not quite the same as ours. If you wish, you can get a free leaflet describing the sounds of foreign telephone tones from British Telecom. Dial 100 and ask for Freefone BTI. To telephone Britain from Austria or Germany you need to dial 00, then pause a moment to be connected, followed by 44 and then your STD code (but leave out the first 0 of the STD code) and finally your own number.

If you ring a friend staying in another German/Austrian/Swiss family, you will find that whoever answers the telephone will say: "Hallo, hier . . ." and give their name, or else they'll just say their surname. You can ask them: "Ist . . . da?" giving your friend's name.

If you need to make a phone call from a public call box, keep a supply of small coins. The instructions are explained in pictures, and the coins you need will be illustrated.

Mealtimes

Germans eat a good breakfast!

Lunch is usually the largest meal of the day and can be as early as midday. In the north of Germany people eat potatoes and hot vegetables with their meat, as is the custom in Britain, but in the south and in Austria a separate side salad is more likely to be served, sometimes before the main meal starts.

If you are vegetarian it might be a good idea to let your host family know in good time. Maybe you could write and tell them in advance. The following phrases might help you to explain if there are some foods you'd rather avoid:

Ich bin Vegetarier(in). *I'm vegetarian.*

Ich esse kein Fleisch/keinen Fisch/keine Eier. *I don't eat meat/fish/ eggs.*

Normalerweise esse ich keinen Käse, keine Butter und keine Milch. *I don't usually eat cheese, butter or milk.*

Ich nehme nur Gemüse/Salat. *Just the vegetables/salad, please.*

Ich esse Senf/Öl nicht gern. *I don't like mustard/oil.*

Ohne Soße/Essig, bitte. *Without gravy/vinegar, please.*

In the south they are also more likely to serve large dumplings, called **Nockerl** or **Kloß**, or pasta with a hot meal, rather than potatoes. Chips are also popular. One speciality is **Spätzle**, a sort of noodle, which is very filling. You may find that there are not as many filling vegetables served with fish or meat as we are used to, but that plenty of bread or a dish of dumplings is served instead.

   Later in the afternoon you may have a piece of cake or tart and a drink. This is known as **Kaffee und Kuchen**, or in Austria as a **Jause**. Sometimes tea is served with cream or long-life milk instead of fresh milk and if you don't like that you could try it on its own (**Schwarzer Tee**) or with lemon instead; it's quite refreshing.

Ich möchte Tee ohne Sahne, bitte, aber mit Zitrone. *I'd like tea without cream but with lemon.*

Fitting In

> Your evening meal may not be a cooked dinner, but more like an English high tea, and not eaten very late.

If you are served something unusual and are not sure how to eat it, watch what the others do, then copy them discreetly! However they may invite you to start first:

Bedien' dich!   *Serve yourself!*

Greif' bitte zu!   *Please help yourself!*

Fang' bitte an!   *Do begin!*

Then you'll have to ask:

Wie ißt man das?   *How does one eat that?*

If you are not told to start right away, wait until one of the adults begins to eat, then you know that you won't be thought rude.

> At the start of a meal Germans wish each other **Guten Appetit!** – enjoy your meal. The Austrians say, **Mahlzeit!** You reply with the same words. And don't be surprised if you are out picnicking to find passers-by wishing you, **Guten Appetit!** or **Mahlzeit!**; most Germans and Austrians are friendly to strangers. They will also wish you, **'Tag** or **Grüß Gott** (or **Grüezi** in Switzerland) when they pass you while out walking.

Accepting and declining food

You may be offered food which you've never tasted before. Do try everything, otherwise you might miss something really delicious. But if you feel unsure about it, ask to be served with just a small portion:

- **Nur ein bißchen, bitte.** *Only a little bit, please.*
- **Darf ich ein bißchen probieren, bitte?** *May I try a little, please?*
- ▶ **Ich habe das noch nie gegessen; darf ich nur ein bißchen haben?** *I've never eaten that before; may I have just a little bit?*

Then if you like it:

Ja, das schmeckt mir gut. *Yes, that tastes good.*

Ja, mir schmeckt's gut. *Yes, that's tasty.*

Das schmeckt vorzüglich/ausgezeichnet/sehr gut. *That tastes superb/excellent/very good.*

If you'd like a little more:

Noch ein bißchen, bitte. *A little more, please.*

But if you didn't like it:

Das esse ich nicht gern. *I don't enjoy eating that.*

Ach, das hat mir nicht geschmeckt. *Ugh, I don't like the taste.*

However, if you are allergic to something and are unable to eat it:

- **Ich bin allergisch gegen . . .** *I'm allergic to . . .*
- ▶ **Ich kann das nicht essen, ich habe eine Allergie dagegen.** *I can't eat that, I'm allergic to it.*

If it is noticed that you are struggling to finish, someone may say to you:

Du brauchst nicht alles zu essen. *You needn't eat it all.*

Du mußt nicht alles essen. *You don't have to eat it all.*

Then you can give in with gratitude if it was too much for you! If there's something you really do like but you're offered more than you can manage, you may have to say:

Das hat mir sehr geschmeckt, aber ich bin satt! *I really enjoyed that but I'm full up!*

You may be lucky and be asked what you enjoy eating and drinking at the beginning of your stay:

Was ißt du gern und was trinkst du gern?

Then you could reply, listing all your favourite foods and drinks, which you could learn before leaving home:

Ich esse/trinke . . . gern.

Also learn the names of the things you really do dislike!

Ich esse/trinke . . . gar nicht!   *I don't like eating . . . at all!*

Here are some of the foods that have different names in Austria:

Austrian	German	English
Paradeis	**Tomate**	*tomato*
Erdapfel	**Kartoffel**	*potato*
Schlagobers	**Sahne**	*cream*
Marille	**Aprikose**	*apricot*
Palatschinken	**Pfannkuchen**	*pancakes*
Nockerl	**Kloß**	*dumpling* (savoury)

There are also sweet dumplings, called **Knödel** in both countries; however a **Knödel** can also be savoury!

Drinks

Freshly brewed coffee is usually served at the end of a meal or with Kaffee und Kuchen. Tea is not as usual as it is in our country; if you look along the supermarket shelves you'll notice that a great many packets of tea bags are herbal teas. If you do not fancy herbal tea, you could warn your hostess:

Ich trinke Kräutertee/Früchtetee nicht gern. *I don't like herbal tea.*

If you want ordinary tea, ask for:

ein schwarzer Tee mit Milch/Zitrone, bitte.

> Fresh fruit juice is common and orange, apple or blackcurrant juice may be served diluted with chilled effervescent mineral water, which is most refreshing in hot weather. In southern and western Germany apple juice with mineral water is known as **Apfelschorle** or **Apfelsaftschorle**.

In Austria, **Spritzer** is popular. It is wine mixed with mineral water or with other drinks such as Coca Cola, and is refreshing, too. **Sprudel** means a fizzy drink and so does **Limonade**. If you would like lemonade, ask for **Sprite** and if you'd like orangeade, you need to ask for **Orangen-Limonade**. Note that the Germans call Coca Cola and Pepsi Cola **Cola**. If you ask for Coke or Pepsi you may be met with blank stares!

When ordering it is usual to ask for **Einmal . . . bitte**, rather than make a long, involved sentence detailing the number of bottles or glasses you would like.

Take care with "Danke"!

> **"Danke"** is short for **"Nein danke"**, so if you want to accept what is being offered to you, say, **"Ja bitte"** or **"Ja gerne"**.
> Remember that **"Bitte"** on its own can mean, **"Pardon?"** or **"Help yourself"** , **"Here you are"** or **"Can I help you?"** as well as **"Please"** – it's a very useful word!

Money-back bottles

The Germans are ecologically very aware and try to recycle as much as they can. More drinks are sold in bottles than in cans and, to encourage the return of these bottles, many have 10 Pfennig, 15 Pfennig or 30 Pfennig money back offers. If the bottle is printed or embossed with, **Pfand-wert-Flasche**, you know you'll get some money back when you return it. From some shops you will receive a token instead of money. This token can be used towards another purchase, but it doesn't have to be another drink. Ring-pull cans are not very common. If you think you'll need to buy a bottled drink while you're on an outing, take a bottle opener with you. If you buy a bottled drink in a self-service café, you will find a bottle opener by the till. Customers open their bottles while waiting for their change.

The legal age for buying alcohol is lower than in Britain and in some parts of Germany people drink beer as a matter of course, the way English people proverbially drink tea!

Noch ein Bier?

Each town or area has its own local brewery, some producing very mild beers, but take heed! Some that look like harmless lagers are, in fact, very potent! However, there is no "macho" image to beer drinking and people are just as likely to have a fizzy drink or mineral water as their second drink, or even their first, so you don't have to feel embarrassed if you don't enjoy alcoholic drinks. You might say:

Ich trinke lieber Saft. *I'd prefer to drink fruit juice.*

Ich trinke lieber einen Sprudel. *I'd prefer a fizzy drink.*

If you are in the south in winter you could be offered the equivalent of a hot toddy made with warm fruit juice laced with a fruit brandy – most heart-warming after being out in the snow – or a **Glühwein** which is hot red wine flavoured with spice.

The end of the meal

At the end of the meal you might like to say thanks if you really enjoyed the food, and you might want to offer to help:

Vielen Dank, das schmeckte mir sehr gut. *Thanks a lot, that tasted nice.*

Darf ich Ihnen helfen? *May I help you?*

Daily Life

Sometimes it's hard to find topics of conversation, especially at the beginning of your stay when you don't know the family well. Here are some things you could take that would help you start a conversation and break the ice:

- photos of your family, pets, house;
- an illustrated booklet about your home area;
- a map showing the area where you live;
- leaflets about places of interest near you;
- books about the Royal Family, London, our countryside;
- magazines on a subject that interests you (pop music, films, computers, stamps, bird watching etc).

This will give you the chance to show you're keen to speak German, even if what you can say is rather limited. Before you leave home you could practise describing your family and hobbies.

Another idea to help break the ice is to take an individual gift for your partner, in addition to the family present. Sweets are often quite different in other countries and some ideas which are typical of Britain are: hot peppermints, fudge, liquorice allsorts, butterscotch or Turkish delight. A book can provide a good opening for a chat. If you know that your partner has a particular interest or hobby, such as music, ballet, pets, railways, aircraft, cars, horses, computers, handicrafts, fashion, pop groups or film stars, an illustrated book or magazine on that subject would give you both something to discuss.

If you don't know of any special interest, a humorous book of cartoons would provide some fun – but take care to choose one that's easy to understand, otherwise you may have difficulty explaining complicated jokes and puns in German!

Occupying yourself

Card games, chess, draughts, dominoes, Scrabble, Mastermind – all these cross the language barrier; so if you have a pocket set it would be a good idea to take it with you.

A pack of cards has the advantage that you can fill in any spare moments with a few games of Patience, especially if your partner is occupied with school work and the rest of the family is busy.

It's also a good idea to take with you a couple of paperbacks for those times when you want to be on your own to relax. You won't find television or radio as restful as at home because you'll have to concentrate to understand, although it is funny when well-known British or American series appear dubbed in German!

Going to school

Sometimes school exchanges are arranged so that you spend a few days with your partner in their school. Don't be daunted by the thought of all those lessons conducted in German – it is quite entertaining to have a maths or physics lesson in another language and of course you don't have to give the answers!

Although the pupils abroad don't have to wear a uniform, they are expected to attend school looking neat and tidy. Often casual clothes are worn, including jeans, as long as they're not scruffy, but check with your partner if you're not sure what is suitable:

Darf ich diese Jeans anziehen?   *May I put these jeans on?*

Darf ich diese Jeans tragen?   *May I wear those jeans?* (If already on.)

Soll ich etwas schönes anziehen?   *Should I wear something smart?*

Soll ich mich fein machen?   *Should I dress up?*

Brauche ich heute . . .
  . . . ein Blouson?
  . . . eine Sonnenbrille?
  . . . einen Regenschirm/Regenmantel?

Today do I need . . .
  . . . a jacket?
  . . . sunglasses?
  . . . an umbrella/a raincoat?

Schools in Germany and Austria can start as early as 8 o'clock and lessons continue until lunchtime with only short breaks in between sessions. Students from outlying areas have to leave home extremely early and so would be starving part way through the morning! The children usually bring with them a **zweites Frühstück**. In Austria they call it a **Jausebrot** or just a **Jause**. It consists of rolls, chocolate and/or fruit to eat between lessons. If you are given an elevenses by your partner's mother, don't forget to take it with you, otherwise you'll be ravenous by the time you eventually get back from school!

Going out

If you travel badly and feel sick in a car or coach, take a tablet before you leave. If you have none, explain:

- Ich fühle mich krank in einem Auto. Haben Sie eine Reisetablette, bitte? *I get car sick. Have you a travel pill, please?*

▶ Ich nehme normalerwiese eine Reisetablette; können Sie mir bitte eine Tablette geben? *I usually take a travel pill; could you please give me a tablet?*

▶ Mir wird beim Autofahren schlecht, deshalb nehme ich normalerweise Reisetabletten. Könnten Sie mir bitte eine geben? *I get ill on car journeys so I usually take travel pills. Could you please give me one?*

If you really dislike swallowing tablets it's possible to get anti-travel sickness chewing gum called **Reise-kaugummi-dragées**.

While you're on a school exchange some of the group outings may be by coach and you might be allowed to go off on your own. Should the instructions to meet again be given in German by the teacher from the host school, do listen carefully to make sure you know where and when to meet up. Take care if the time is given in the 24 hour clock (most usual in Germany, Austria and Switzerland) and ask, to double check, if you're unsure:

Un wieviel Uhr fahren wir zurück? *What time do we travel back?*

Wir treffen wir uns um sechzehn Uhr, nicht um sechs Uhr dreißig

Beware of the following!

> **Halb zwei** means half to two – we'd say *half past one*. In Austria and some parts of Germany you'll hear **Viertel fünf** which means a quarter on the way to five. We'd say *a quarter past four*. If in doubt, query:

Viertel nach fünf oder Viertel vor fünf?   *A quarter past four or quarter to four?*

Vier Uhr fünfzehn oder vier Uhr fünfundvierzig?   *Four fifteen or four forty-five?*

> You might also hear: **Drei Viertel fünf** which means three quarters on the way to five. We'd say *a quarter to five*, or *four forty-five*. To check you have understood the correct time you could ask:

Viertel vor fünf?   *A quarter to five?*

Vier Uhr fünfundvierzig?   *Four forty-five?*

Your host family is quite likely to take you to meet friends or relatives, where **Kaffee und Kuchen** are often served. If you don't enjoy coffee, don't be afraid to ask for tea or a soft drink instead:

Entschuldigen Sie, ich trinke nicht gern Kaffee, aber ich trinke Tee/Fruchtsaft/Mineralwasser/Sprudel.   *I'm sorry, I don't enjoy coffee, but I do drink tea/fruit juice/mineral water/fizzy drinks.*

If you have to meet up again at the coach, look at it carefully so that you'll recognise it! Make sure you can remember where it is parked and make a note of its make, colour and number if you think you might not be sure of identifying the correct one. A good plan is to stay with at least one other person all the time.

There will be plenty of hand shaking and people will want to ask you about your family and home town. You could take along with you pictures or booklets about your home area, this would make conversation easier for you. You could also talk about what you are interested in:

Ich interessiere mich für Fußball/Fotografie/Pferde. *I'm keen on football/photography/horses.*

Out and About

Feste are held in the summer or early autumn and are similar to an English summer fête and a fair. There is a really friendly atmosphere, with brass bands playing and often a pop group, too.

There will be lots of stalls selling hot dogs and many other sorts of hot sausages (rather than hamburgers or beefburgers, as we have in England). **Bockwurst** are boiled sausages and **Bratwurst** are fried ones. You won't find tea or coffee on sale, but there will be stalls selling different kinds of locally brewed beer, as well as plenty of fizzy dinks, especially Coca Cola.

The **Fest** usually goes on after dark and may end with a magnificent firework display. If you hear your partner talk of a **Vergnügungspark**, you know there will be a fairground there, too, so you'll need to take some money if you want to go on any of the rides. At some **Feste**, local clubs hold sideshows to raise money so you might want to take some change with you to try your luck at hoop-la and so on.

If you have to walk home afterwards, you'll need a sweater with you, as even at midsummer it can get chilly around midnight! Apart from going to the opera or the theatre in the city, nobody dresses formally but if you need to check what to wear ask:

Was soll ich tragen? *What shall I wear?*

Sports

The majority of Germans are keen on sporting activities. You might be asked about the sports that you enjoy:

Spielst du gern Tennis/Fußball/Volleyball/Tischtennis/Golf/Badminton (also known as Federballspiel?) *Do you enjoy playing tennis/ football/volleyball/table tennis/golf/badminton?*

Tanzest/Schwimmst du gern? *Do you enjoy dancing/swimming?*

Fährst du gern Ski/Rad? *Do you enjoy skiing/cycling?*

Or you could be asked whether you're good at something:

Spielst du gut Tennis/Fußball usw.? *Do you play tennis/football etc. well?*

Fährst du gut Ski? *Do you ski well?*

Schwimmst/Reitest du gut? *Do you swim well/ride well?*

Or you could be asked whether you know how to do these things:

Kannst du schwimmen/tanzen/reiten/Ski fahren/Tennis spielen? *Can you swim/dance/ride/ski/play tennis?*

You may need replies similar to these:

Ich kann schwimmen/tanzen/reiten/kegeln. *I can swim/dance/ride/ play ten-pin bowling.*

Ich möchte Ski fahren (or Ski laufen)/Schlittschuh laufen/Hockey spielen/Skilanglauf treiben. *I'd like to go skiing/skating/play hockey/ go cross country skiing.*

Ich spiele sehr gut/ziemlich gut/nicht sehr gut/nur etwas . . . *I play . . . very well/quite well/not very well/only a bit.*

Ich schwimme/tanze/reite/kegele gut/ein bißchen/wirklich sehr gut. *I can swim/dance/ride/bowl well/a little/really very well.*

Ich schwimme usw. wirklich sehr gern/furchtbar gern. *I really enjoy/thoroughly enjoy swimming etc.*

However, if you're not the sporty type, don't know how to play a particular game or don't feel in the mood, you might find the following sentences of use:

Ich schwimme/tanze/reite nicht gern. *I don't enjoy swimming/ dancing/riding.*

Ich spiele gar nicht gern Golf/Hockey. *I don't like playing golf/ hockey at all!*

Ich laufe überhaupt nicht gern Ski/Schlittschuh! *I can't bear skiing/ skating!*

Ich kann nicht . . . *I don't know how to . . .*

Ich will heute nicht . . . *I don't want to . . . today.*

But if you don't want to seem like a spoilsport, you could tell your partner what you would like to do instead, for instance:

Heute ist es sehr heiß; ich möchte nicht Tennis spielen, aber ich spiele gern Minigolf. *It's so hot today; I wouldn't like to play Tennis, but I'd like to play miniature golf.*

Ich spiele nicht gern Hockey, ich spiele lieber Volleyball. *I don't enjoy hockey, I'd prefer volleyball.*

If you go swimming in the public baths you'll find it's usual for people to wear a bathing cap. If you haven't got a swimming hat you'll probably be able to borrow or hire one at the pool.

Muß ich eine Badekappe (in Austria eine Badehaube) tragen? *Do I have to wear a bathing hat?*

Ich brauche eine Badekappe (Badehaube). *I need a bathing cap.*

Kann ich eine Badekappe (Badehaube) borgen/leihen? *Am I able to borrow/hire a swimming cap?*

Would you rather stay at home?

Your partner may have made plans to go out but then realises that you're too tired or not feeling up to going out after all. Then somebody might say:

Du brauchst nicht mitzukommen. *You don't have to come along.*

If that is a relief to you and you'd rather stay behind:

Danke, ich bleibe zu Hause. *Thanks, I'll stay at home.*

But if you actually do want to go too:

Nein, das geht; ich komme gern mit. *No, that's fine; I'd like to come along.*

Shopping

You might need to ask for shops that you need if you're out shopping on your own:

Wo ist die Apotheke? *Where's the chemist?* (medical)

Wo ist die Drogerie/der Drogist? *Where is the chemist?* (general)

Wo ist die Parfumerie? *Where is the perfumery?* (specialist perfume shop, but dearer than G.B.)

Wo ist der Supermarkt? *Where's the supermarket?*

Wo ist die Bäckerei? *Where's the baker?*

Wo kann man hier Andenken kaufen? *Where can one buy souvenirs?*

Wo kann man Ansichtskarten kaufen? *Where can one buy picture postcards?*

Ich möchte etwas für meine Familie kaufen. *I'd like to buy something for my family.*

Ich möchte etwas nicht zu Teures kaufen. *I'd like to buy something that's not too expensive.*

Out and About

Although big stores stay open all day, smaller shops still close for one or two hours for lunch, and so do banks. While you are out shopping you might want to stop for a snack. If the family have treated you to lots of things and you feel you'd like to repay them you might want to use some of the sentences below:

Könnten wir hier eine Pause machen und etwas trinken/essen/ein Eis essen? *Can we stop here for a drink/snack/an ice?*

- **Soll ich zahlen?** *Shall I pay?*
- **Darf ich zahlen?** *May I pay?*
- **Lassen Sie mich bitte diesmal zahlen? (to adults)**
- **Lass' mich bitte 'mal zahlen.** *Do let me pay this time.*

Make sure that if you do go out shopping on your own, you know the way back. You could carry a card with your host family's address and telephone number on it and you could ask your partner to draw on the back a sketch map of the route from the house to the shops.

Money

Instead of having all your money in foreign currency, you could take some travellers' cheques from the bank or building society.

It can be convenient to take a mixture of £10 and £5 travellers' cheques so that you have high values to cash at the start of your holiday and lower values if you only need to cash a small amount towards the end of your stay.

Remember to keep your money in a safe pocket. Don't carry much more money than you'll need each day – unfortunately pickpockets are an international menace.

Buying and Paying

You'll probably visit interesting and unusual places during your stay and it's a nice idea to buy slide photos (**Diapositiven**) or postcards (**Ansichtskarten**) as mementos. Remember to ask for **Ansichtskarten** and not **Postkarten** if you want view cards, as **Postkarten** are plain white cards, often sold ready stamped.

If choosing anything else as a memento make sure that it is neither too fragile, too bulky nor too heavy to pack for the journey home.

Keep your purchases easily accessible when you finally pack, as the customs officers may wish to check. The best thing to do is to make a list of all that you buy, with the price, and then this list can be shown if necessary. Don't forget that if you're under eighteen you must not bring in cigarettes or alcohol, not even as a gift, and on no account bring any sort of fireworks. If you are in any doubt about whether you should buy something, check with an adult. You would be most unpopular with your group if you were the cause of everyone being detained, as you could be held up for hours!

Postage

When you buy postcards, it's almost always possible to buy stamps at the same place (or in the **Tabak**) because postage for cards to Britain is the same as internal German postage. Letters, however, cost more to send, so you'll need to go to the Post Office. If you need to ask the way:

Wo ist das Postamt/die Post? *Where is the Post Office?*

At the Post Office counter you'll need to ask:

Wieviel kostet ein Brief nach England? *How much is a letter to England?*

Ich brauche eine Briefmarke zu . . . Pfennig. *I need a . . . pfennig stamp.*

Ich brauche 2/3/4 Briefmarken zu . . . Pfennig. *I need 2/3/4 . . . pfennig stamps.*

In the shops

Although supermarkets and many big chemists and souvenir shops are self-service, there are still a great many small family businesses and there you may be greeted with:

Guten Tag, kann ich Ihnen helfen?   *Good day, may I help you?*

Guten Tag, was darf es sein?   *Good day, what would you like?*

Be brave and don't shirk the opportunity to talk in German!

Ich schaue mich nur um.   *I'm just looking around.*

Ich weiß es nicht genau.   *I'm not really sure.*

Darf ich das anprobieren?   *May I try it on?*

Haben Sie dasselbe eine Nummer größer/kleiner?   *Do you have this in a larger/smaller size?*

Haben Sie diese Art aus Nylon/Leder/Wolle/Baumwolle/Leinen/Seide?   *Do you have this in nylon/leather/wool/cotton/linen/silk?*

Das paßt mir gut.   *That suits me.*

Das paßt mir nicht gut.   *That doesn't suit me.*

Das gefällt mir. Ich nehme das.   *I do like that. I'll take it.*

You may also be asked whether you need anything else:

Sonst noch etwas?
Darf es noch etwas sein?
Haben Sie sonst noch einen Wunsch?

But if you've got all you need:

Nein, danke, das ist alles. Wieviel kostet das?/kosten sie?

Luckily you won't need to worry about the price being spoken too quickly for you to catch the amount; modern tills display the cost to the customer as well as the cashier, so you can easily read the display and sort out your notes and coins ready to pay.

It's worth remembering that back in England you can't change foreign coins back into sterling and the majority of the cross-Channel ferries don't take Swiss, Austrian or German money. Unless you collect foreign coins or are planning a return trip, you should try to use up as much **Kleingeld** as you can during your last day or two.

Travelling on your own

If you use public transport on your own, look at the name at the top of the bus or tram stop when you get on. Each stop is named, for example, **Markt**, **Hauptbahnhof** or **Kristuskirche** and then you know which stop to ask for on your return.

However, if you're not sure where to get off, enter at the front of the vehicle and explain to the driver:

Ich möchte zum Zentrum/zur Kristuskirche/zum Bahnhof fahren. Wo muß ich aussteigen? *I need the town centre/Christ Church/the station. Where should I get off?*

You can either buy your ticket in advance from an automatic machine or enter the bus or tram at the front and buy your ticket from the driver.

Ich möchte zum Marktplatz, wieviel kostet das? *How much is it to the market place?*

Eine Fahrkarte zum Schloß, bitte. *A ticket to the castle, please.*

Einmal/Zweimal/Dreimal zum Dom. *One/Two/Three to the cathedral.*

> If you buy your ticket from a machine you'll find that it is not date-stamped. To validate the ticket for your journey, enter the tram or bus by the centre door and poke your ticket into the machine by the centre aisle; this will date stamp it. There is also a machine at the front by the driver, in case anyone needs to get on there to ask the driver a question, although they already have a ticket. Don't be tempted to travel with an invalid ticket, in the hope that you can use it again and again! Ticket inspectors are very thorough, fairly frequent and in plain clothes!

If you're eligible for a child's fare you may have to prove your age by showing something with your date of birth on it, like a YHA card or your passport, but keep them somewhere safe while you carry them around.

Minor Mishaps

There are certain simple precautions you can take to look after yourself and to make sure that a minor problem does not turn into a major worry for you and your hosts.

Medicines are, of course, available in other countries, although German, Austrian and Swiss medicines are very expensive. The other problem might be in obtaining those you are used to and which you know work for you. This is *not* the time to try out new medicines, skin creams, etc; you might be allergic to them and this will increase your problems.

You should also take with you any medicines which you have to take regularly for conditions such as asthma, hay fever, migraines. Take these with you even if you think that it is not the time of year when you usually need them. Conditions like asthma and hay fever may be triggered off by some plant or substance you haven't come across before. If you have room, you could also take some, or all, of the following: a few pain-killers; a selection of sticking plasters; indigestion tablets; throat sweets; a small tube of antiseptic cream and an anti-diarrhoea preparation.

Hopefully you won't need anything for an upset stomach as food is very fresh and all tap water is drinkable in Germany, Austria and Switzerland. However, the change in water or diet may affect you. In the case of diarrhoea (**Durchfall**) take a dose of a preparation such as "Arret", which is available as pills or as a mixture. (Pills are easier to pack and carry.)

If you should suffer from constipation (**Verstopfung**) you need to drink plenty of water or fruit juice and treat yourself to some dried fruit or wholemeal biscuits or crispbread. Wholemeal digestive biscuits (**Vollkornbutterkeks**) are effective and pleasant. Study the packaging and look for the word for roughage, which is **Ballaststoffe** – if the product contains plenty, then that's the thing for you!

In case of illness

If you do feel ill, the following will help you to explain your symptoms or ask for the treatment you need:

Was fehlt dir? *What's the matter?*

Ich bin krank. *I'm ill.*

Es tut mir weh! *It hurts!*

Ich habe . . .	*I have . . .*
. . . **Kopfschmerzen.**	. . . *a headache.*
. . . **Halsschmerzen.**	. . . *a sore throat.*
. . . **Zahnschmerzen.**	. . . *toothache.*
. . . **Magenschmerzen.**	. . . *stomachache.*
. . . **Ohrenschmerzen.**	. . . *earache.*
. . . **Fieber.**	. . . *a high temperature.*
. . . **Durchfall.**	. . . *diarrhoea.*
. . . **Verstopfung.**	. . . *constipation.*

Ich huste viel. *I'm coughing a lot.*

Mir ist schwindlig. *I feel giddy.*

Meine Hand tut weh. *My hand hurts.*

Mein Bauch/Knie/Dein tut weh. *My stomach/knee/leg hurts.*

Ich habe mich verbrannt. *I've burnt myself.*

Ich habe mich geschnitten. *I've cut myself.*

Es ist ein stechender/dumpfer/stichartiger/leichter/starker Schmerz. *It's a sharp/dull/shooting/slight/severe pain.*

Ich brauche . . .	*I need . . .*
. . . **Aspirin.**	. . . *aspirin.*
. . . **Halspastillen.**	. . . *throat tablets.*
. . . **Hansaplast/Pflaster.**	. . . *sticking plasters.*
. . . **Salbe (gegen/für Insekten-**	. . . *ointment (for insect bites).*
stiche).	
(gegen/für Sonnenbrand).	*(for sunburn).*

... Hustensaft.	... *cough syrup.*
... Hustenbonbons.	... *cough sweets.*
... Monatsbinden/Binden.	... *sanitary towels.*
... Tampons.	... *tampons.*
... etwas für empfindliche Lippen.	... *something for sore lips.*
... eine Packung medizinische Halspastillen.	... *a packet of medicated throat lozenges.*
... eine Packung antimikrobielle/antibakterielle Pastillen.	... *a packet of anti-bacterial lozenges.*

If you do get ill, we hope that very soon you'll be able to say:

- Ich fühle mich viel besser.   *I feel much better.*

▶ Ich fühle mich heute wirklich viel besser und Sie brauchen sich keine Sorgen zu machen.   *Today I'm really feeling very much better and you don't need to worry about me.*

Medical instructions you might encounter:

Die Tabletten in Wasser zerfallen/auflösen lassen.   *Dissolve the tablets in water.*

Mehrmals täglich 1–2 Tabletten langsam im Mund zergehen lassen.   *Suck 1–2 tablets slowly several times a day.*

Ist trotz richtiger Einnahme nach 2–3 Tagen keine Besserung festzustellen, sollten Sie den Arzt aufsuchen.   *If you don't feel any improvement within 2–3 days of beginning treatment, consult your doctor.*

Going to the doctor

If you should have to go to the doctor remember to take your E111 form with you so that you'll be able to claim back any fees that are payable for your treatment.

Some things the doctor might say to you:

Machen Sie den Mund auf.   *Open wide/Say, "Aaaah!".*

Tief atmen, bitte.   *Breathe deeply, please.*

Husten Sie, bitte.   *Cough, please.*

Ich werde Ihnen ein Antibiotikum verschreiben.   *I'm going to prescribe you an antibiotic.*

Machen Sie den Mund auf

Nehmen Sie 1/2/3 Tabletten mit einem Glas Wasser vor jeder Mahlzeit. *Take 1/2/3 tablets with water before meals.*

Accidental breakages

If you damage or break anything all you can do is apologise profusely and offer to pay to repair or replace the article.

Es tut mir wirklich leid. *I'm terribly sorry.*

Ich werde Ihnen ein neues Glas/eine neue Tasse/einen neuen Teller kaufen. *I'll buy you a new glass/cup/plate.*

Können Sie es reparieren lassen? *Can it be repaired?*

Darf ich zahlen? *May I pay?*

Mending

If you tear anything or lose a button you may need to borrow a needle and thread or ask for help if you can't sew!

- Könnten Sie mir bitte eine Nadel und etwas Garn geben? *Could you let me have a needle and thread?*

▶ Ich habe mein Kleid/meine Hose/meinen Mantel zerrissen, aber ich habe keine Nadel oder Garn. *I've torn my dress/trousers/coat, but I haven't any needle or thread.*

Ich kann nicht nähen. *I don't know how to sew.*

Können Sie bitte mein Kleid/meine Hose/meinen Mantel zunähen? *Could you please sew up my dress/trousers/coat?*

Losing belongings

It is a good idea to mark any belongings with your name. You should take especial care not to forget articles that you put down while out on trips, taking photographs and so on. A carrier bag containing your packed lunch and belongings is easily forgotten in the excitement of photographing something special. A back pack, haversack, small rucksack or a shoulder bag, would be better, as it will leave both your hands free. Inside it keep a card with your name and address, both your home address and your holiday one, then if your bag does get mislaid it will hopefully be returned to you.

It is a good idea to have these addresses inside your wallet, purse, handbag or camera case. Also, make a note of your passport number and the numbers of any traveller's cheques. Keep those numbers somewhere safe and your passport somewhere even safer!

Take great care of it if you have to carry it with you (as proof of your age for cut price tickets or when you go to the bank to cash traveller's cheques). Maybe your host parents would be kind enough to look after your passport for you.

Könnten Sie bitte auf meinen Paß/meine Reisechecks aufpassen? *Please could you look after my passport/traveller's cheques.*

It's a sensible idea not to keep all your money in the same place. Luckily most modern jackets have safe pockets which zip, button or fasten with velcro. Hopefully you won't need to use these:

Ich habe mein/meine/meinen . . . verloren. *I've lost my . . .*

Ich habe mein/meine/meinen . . . vergessen. *I've forgotten my . . .*

If you do lose something of value, tell your host family right away as they will know how to set about informing the police or applying to the lost property office (**Fundbüro**).

Getting Lost

You may have the opportunity to venture out on your own while you are abroad. Don't forget to have with you a card with your host family's name and address. Then if you should lose yourself, you only have to show it (to a shopkeeper, perhaps) and say:

Ich habe mich verirrt. *I've lost my way.*

Ich habe mich verlaufen. *I'm lost.*

Ich suche diese Adresse. *I'm looking for this address.*

Können Sie bitte mir helfen? *Could you help me please?*

Listen very carefully to the directions you are given and repeat any parts you weren't sure of, just to be certain. Remember:

links *left*

rechts *right*

geradeaus *straight on*

Saying No

If there is anything that you don't want to get involved in, you only need to say firmly but politely that you don't want to try:

Nein, danke, ich rauche nicht. *No, thanks, I don't smoke.*

Ich will nicht rauchen, danke. *I don't want to smoke, thanks.*

Nein, danke, ich will kein Bier/keinen Wein trinken. *No, thanks, I don't want a beer/wine.*

Das habe ich nicht gern. *I don't like that.*

Ich will das nicht versuchen, danke. *I don't want to try that, thanks.*

Ich habe keine Lust dazu. *I'm not keen on that.*

Homesickness

This is a perfectly natural feeling, especially if this is your first time away from home. If you do start to feel homesick, there are some things which do help to overcome this sad feeling. However, other things, such as fatigue, aggravate the feeling of homesickness. Things seem much better if you're not tired, so if you are feeling exhausted from hearing, speaking and thinking in German, ask for an early night.

- Ich bin sehr müde and will ins Bett gehen. *I'm very tired and would like to go to bed.*

▶ Ich bin sehr müde und will heute abend früh schlafen. *I'm very tired and I'd like to go to bed early this evening.*

The worst thing of all is to be on your own with nothing to do. Don't mope but get out paper and pen! Writing a long newsy letter home has a marvellously cheering effect.

You may find a quick phone call home cheers you up; but it could also have the opposite effect, and hearing voices from home may leave you more upset. So decide how emotional you feel before ringing home.

Sometimes you may be feeling homesick because, in fact, you're bored. If your partner is reserved and leaves you to your own devices a lot, perhaps you could suggest to your partner, or to a brother or sister, an activity that you would enjoy: a game, a film, a walk, or a visit to a family where one of your own friends is staying.

Möchtest du . . .
... Tennis/Karten/Schach spielen?
... einen Film sehen?
... einen Schaufensterbummel machen?
... meine Freunde/Freundinnen besuchen?
Geht das? *Is that all right?*

Would you like to . . .
... play tennis/cards/chess?
... watch a film?
... go window shopping?
... visit my friends?

If your partner is busy with something, like homework, that you cannot join in, don't just sit in your room feeling lonely. If you don't want to read or listen to the radio or cassettes, you could offer to help the parents:

Darf ich Ihnen helfen? *May I help you?*

Darf ich die Kartoffeln schälen? *May I peel the potatoes?*

But if there is a day when it all gets on top of you and you feel tearful, you can explain:

Ich habe Heimweh. *I'm homesick.*

Ich bin ein bißchen traurig. *I feel rather sad.*

Meine Familie fehlt mir. *I'm missing my family.*

Ich möchte meine Eltern anrufen. *I'd like to phone my parents.*

Of course there are many cases where the British visitors actually prefer living with their host family and don't want to go home! Or they enjoy their visit so much that they return to the same family again and again. We hope that you enjoy your exchange that much, too.

What if you don't fit in?

It isn't very often that an exchange doesn't work – but just in case there are any problems here are some ideas to help you.

If you seem to be ignored, give your partner the benefit of the doubt; he or she may not be moody but only feeling slightly shy or embarrassed. Try approaching him or her with suggestions of what to do. Should people seem withdrawn, it could very well be shyness or just thoughtlessness.

Quite often adults can feel shy or reserved too and this might make them appear stand-offish. A beaming smile from you could help overcome reservations on their part, and once the ice is broken you won't feel left out any more. Perhaps the parents would enjoy joining in a game of cards, too.

However, if you yourself are terribly shy, bravely pluck up courage and smile – it will encourage everyone to make you welcome.

Don't worry if you get on better with a brother or sister than with your partner, that doesn't matter.

If your partner decides to be awkward, sulk or have a family row, slip away so that you don't get drawn into the argument. You could take a copy of *The Growing Pains of Adrian Mole* and laugh about the episode later on.

Try to make some time when you can be on your own. You could go to your room to write postcards, look at magazines or listen to music. Half an hour alone will be restful for you and give the family a chance to talk about personal matters.

Talk to your organisers early on about any problems you feel unable to cope with as they will have the tact and the language to be able to sort things out before they get out of hand.

Finally, remember that when your partner comes to share your home, school and friends, she or he will be experiencing difficulties too. Try to make the visit a happy one and we hope that this exchange will be the start of a lifelong friendship between you and your family and your partner's family.

The End of your stay

Preparing for your return journey

Aber sie hat ihre Hausschuhe vergessen!

Pack in good time – in case you have to repack because you have so many souvenirs to cram in!

If you have never packed for yourself before there is no need to be daunted by the large pile of your belongings and the not as large suitcase! Begin by packing the larger and heavier things at the bottom, heaviest at the back. If you put underwear and hankies into the toes of your shoes it will prevent the shoes getting squashed. Keep any clothes which crease easily and pack those near the top; then everything else needs to be fitted in like a jigsaw. One other tip: clothes which are folded fit in better than those that are screwed up!

Remember to leave out the clean clothes you need for the day you travel home! Check that you haven't left behind your night clothes, slippers, or anything in the bathroom – all so easily done!

Pack any gifts that you've bought safely near the top of your suitcase or in your hand luggage, because a custom's officer may want to see what you have bought abroad. Make a list of any purchases with their prices; you can then show this if you are stopped as you go through the custom's control. Even in the green "Nothing to Declare" channel, spot checks are sometimes carried out.

There are custom's restrictions depending on whether you're under fifteen, under eighteen or adult. If you're travelling in a party, the leader will have a copy of the duty-free allowances and if you travel independently you should receive a leaflet with your ticket. *Never* agree to bring back anything – parcels, bags, packets, bottles – which someone asks you to carry back as a favour, they could be involving you in something illegal. Obviously, this does not apply to any presents your host family may wish you to bring back for your own family. If you are going to buy anything in the duty-free shop, note the prices carefully – sometimes it's cheaper to buy the same thing in one of the big stores back in Britain! You must keep your passport in a safe place, but remember, you will need to show it to the customs officials so it must be handy at all times.

Thanking your host family

To the parents you could say any of these:

- Ich bin Ihnen sehr dankbar.   *I'm very grateful to you.*
- Ich war sehr glücklich bei Ihnen.   *I was very happy with you.*
- Es war ein sehr interessanter Austausch.   *It was a most interesting exchange.*
- ▶ Ich danke Ihnen für einen herrlichen Aufenthalt.   *Thank you for such a lovely stay.*
- ▶ Ich danke Ihnen für Ihre Gastfreundshaft/ Gastfreundlichkeit.   *Thank you for your hospitality/welcome.*
- ▶ Ich danke Ihnen herzlichst für all Ihre Mühe.   *Most grateful thanks for all your trouble.*

The parents may say something like this to you:

Nichts zu danken.   *Don't mention it.*

Es war uns ein Vergnügen.   *The pleasure was all ours.*

To your partner you might want to say some of these:

- **Vielen, vielen Dank.**   *Very many thanks.*
- **Ich danke dir vielmals.**   *Thanks a lot.*
- **Es hat wirklich Spaß gemacht.**   *I've had great fun.*
- **Bis nächstes Mal!**   *Until next time!*
- ▶ **Es hat mir sehr gut gefallen.**   *I really enjoyed myself.*
- ▶ **Es war ein sehr angenehmer Aufenthalt.**   *It was such an enjoyable stay.*
- ▶ **Ich freue mich auf deinen Besuch.**   *I'm looking forward to your visit.*
- ▶ **Bis zum nächsten Mal!**   *Until the next time!*

When the family say their farewells you may hear:

Wir hoffen, du hast dich bei uns wohl gefühlt.   *We hope you felt happy with us.*

Wir hoffen, du hast dich gut amüsiert.   *We hope that you enjoyed yourself.*

Hopefully you'll have had a wonderful time and will want to say:

Ja, sehr!

The family might also say:

Wir hoffen, du wirst uns schreiben.   *We hope you'll write to us.*

Schreib oft!   *Write often!*

Besuch uns mal wieder.   *Come and see us again.*

Du bist immer willkommen bei uns.   *You are always welcome.*

Wir hoffen, du wirst uns bald wiedersehen.   *We hope you'll come and see us again soon.*

Kommst du bald wieder zu uns?   *Will you come again soon?*

If you thoroughly enjoyed yourself and would like to visit again you could reply:

Ich möchte gern herkommen!

The family may send good wishes to the rest of your family:

**Besten Gruß/Schönen Gruß/Viele Grüße an deine Eltern/Geschwister/
Familie.**

Then you could answer that you'll convey their good wishes:

Danke sehr, ich werde es ausrichten.

Favourite food

If there were any particular dishes you especially enjoyed, here's
how to ask for the recipes before you leave:

**. . . hat mir sehr geschmeckt. Können Sie mir bitte das Rezept
geben?**   *I did enjoy . . . Could you give me the recipe?*

A letter of thanks

Soon after your return home you'll probably want to write a letter
thanking your host family. If you really don't enjoy writing letters, the
sentences below will help to make it a quick and easy chore for you!

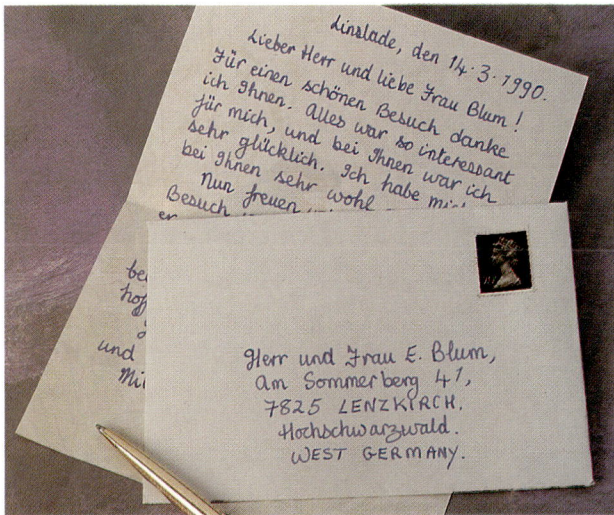

To compose a polite letter to the parents:

Lieber Herr und liebe Frau . . .   *Dear Mr and Mrs . . .*

The End of your stay

Für einen interessanten Besuch danke ich Ihnen. *Thank you for an interesting time.*

Ich habe mich bei Ihnen sehr wohl gefühlt. *I was made so welcome by you.*

Herzlichen Dank für all Ihre Liebe und Sorge. *Grateful thanks for all your kindness and care.*

Alles war so interessant für mich, und bei Ihnen war ich sehr glücklich. *I found everything so interesting and I was very happy with you.*

Recht herzlichen Dank für Ihre Gastfreundschaft und die zusätzliche Mühe. *Most grateful thanks for your hospitality and all the extra work.*

Ich hoffe, daß ich mal wiederkomme. *I hope that I can come again one day.*

You could sign off with:

Mit freundlichen Wünsche/Grüße ... *With best wishes from ...*

Meine Eltern lassen Sie vielmals grüßen. *My parents send their good wishes.*

When you write to your partner some of these sentences may help. Remember in a letter to use a capital letter to begin Du, Dich, Dir and Dein, and also Ihr, Euch and Euer (if you need the plural friendly form to write to the brothers and sisters too).

Herzlichen Dank für eine interessante Zeit. *Many thanks for an interesting time.*

Ich habe mich sehr wohl gefühlt. *I felt really welcomed.*

Ich wünschte, ich hätte länger bei Dir bleiben können. *I wished I could have stayed longer with you.*

Ich freue mich darauf, Dich und Deine Familie wiederzusehen. *I should love to see you all again.*

Ich freue mich auf Deinen Besuch. *I'm looking forward to your visit.*

Bis auf weiteres alles Gute. *All the best until the next time.*

Bis bald! *See you soon.*

Auf Wiedersehen. *Until the next letter!*

Viele Grüße! *Best wishes!*

Tchüß! *Cheers/Bye!*

Appendix

Checklist of essentials to pack

Passport
German/Austrian money and traveller's cheques
E111 Certificate
Enough spare underwear
Nightwear, slippers or soft shoes
Dressing gown or bathrobe if not too bulky
Casual (not scruffy!) clothes
One 'smart' outfit
One pair waterproof shoes
Waterproof coat, anorak or cagoule
A warm sweater
Handkerchiefs or tissues
Small first-aid kit
For girls, sanitary towels or tampons, even if you think you don't
    need them
Small amount of writing paper and envelopes
A pen
Gifts for your exchange family
Addresses of friends or relatives you want to send postcards to
Home phone number or number of friend or neighbour
The name, address and telephone number of your exchange family
Phone number and address in Germany of your trip organiser
A book to read
Playing cards, solitaire or other small game
This book!

Leave at home

Your address and telephone number in Germany and the family's
name
Name, address and telephone number of your trip organiser.

Sizes

Shoe and garment sizes in Germany, Austria and Switzerland differ
from the ones we use in Britain. Below are some tables to help you
choose the nearest equivalent size. US sizing is becoming more
common, especially for sports shoes and clothing. US sizes are
similar, but not always identical, to ours so it's wise to try on anything
you intend to buy.

Shoes

British	2	3	4	5	6	7	8	9	10	11	12
German	35	36	37	38	39	41	42	43	44	45	46

Collar sizes

British	14	14½	15	15½	16	16½	17
German	36	37	38	39	40	41	42

Dresses

British	8	10	12	14	16	18
German	34	36	38	40	42	44

Sweaters

British	32″	34″	36″	38″	40″	42″	44″
German	80cm	86cm	91cm	97cm	102cm	107cm	112cm

Height

British	5′2″	5′4″	5′6″	5′8″	5′10″	6′	6′2″	6′4″
Metric	157	163	168	173	178	182	187	192

Useful Comments and Exclamations

Ways of saying ''Brilliant!'', ''Fantastic!'', ''Great!'' etc:

Ausgezeichnet! **Wunderbar!** **Prima!** **Klasse!**
Fantastisch! **Großartig!** **Super!** **Wunderschön!**

Good wishes:

Alles Gute!   *All the best!*
Viel Glück!   *Good luck!*
Viel Spaß!   *Have fun!*
Viel Vergnügen!   *Have a good time!*
Gute Reise!   *Have a good journey!*
Gute Besserung!   *Get well soon!*
Komm' gut Heim/nach Hause.   *Have a safe journey home.*
Alles Gute zum Geburtstag.   *Happy birthday.*
Fröhliche Weihnachten.   *Happy Christmas.*

Ways of saying grateful thanks:

Danke schön!	**Besten Dank!**
Danke sehr!	**Danke vielmals!**
Vielen Dank!	**Recht vielen Dank!**
Recht herzlichen Dank!	**Vielen Dank noch einmal!**

Don't mention it:

Bitte, bitte.   **Nichts zu danken.**   **Gern geschehen.**

Ways to say: "Really!", "Indeed!" etc:

Ach so!   **Wirklich!**   **Tatsächlich!**   **Echt!**

Answering queries in the positive:

Angenehm.   *Pleased to meet you.*
Sehr erfreut.   *Glad to know you.*
Ja, das geht.   *That's okay.*
Das ist in Ordnung.   *That's all right.*
Das stimmt.   *That's fine.*
Ja, das ist möglich.   *Yes that's possible.*
Das ist eine ausgezeichnete Idee!   *An excellent idea.*
Ja, ich hätte gern ...   *Yes I'd like ...*

Ways of saying "Of course", "Naturally" etc:

Sicher!   **Freilich!**   **Natürlich!**   **Selbsverständlich!**

To show that you're impressed:

Es ist ...   *It's ...*

   ... erstaunlich   *... astonishing*

   ... herrlich   *... magnificent*

   ... eindrucksvoll   *... impressive*

   ... hervorragend   *... superb*

Answering queries in the negative:

Das geht nicht.   *It's not okay.*

Nein, es tut mir leid.   *No, I'm sorry.*

Das ist nicht möglich.   *That's not possible.*

Das ist unmöglich.   *It's impossible.*

Auf keinen Fall.   *Under no circumstances.*

Gar nicht.   *Never.*

Keineswegs.   *No way.*

Überhaupt nicht.   *Not at all.*

Leider/Unglücklicherweise.   *Unfortunately.*

Es ist mir langweilig.   *That's boring.*

Dabei wird mir langweilig.   *I'd find that boring.*

Mir reicht's.   *I've had enough.*

Das geht mir auf die Nerven.   *That gets on my nerves.*

Notice that the Germans often use a negative where we would say something like, "Fine, that's okay":

Kein Problem!   *No problem!*

Keine schlechte Idee.   *Not a bad idea.*

Warum nicht?   *Why not?*

Other comments you might need:

Ja, Moment, bitte./Momentmal, bitte.   *Just a moment, please.*

...ja...   ...er...um...

O weh!   *Oh dear!*

Entschuldigen Sie die Störung.   *Sorry to disturb you.*

Furchtbar!   *Awful!*

Unerhört!   *Terrible/Unheard of!*

Es tut mir leid.   *I'm sorry.*

Verzeihung.   *I beg your pardon.*

Entschuldigen Sie/Entschuldigung.   *Excuse me.*

Gestatten Sie.   *May I (pass)?*

Queries you may need:

Geht das?   *Is that all right?*

Darf ich...?   *May I...?*

Kann ich...?   *Can I...?*

Brauche ich...?   *Do I need...?*

Ich kann nicht...   *I cannot/don't know how to...*

Um wieviel Uhr?   *At what time/When?*

Wo bekomme ich...?   *Where do I catch/get...?* (transport)

Wie weit ist es?   *Har far is it?*

Wie komme ich dorthin?   *How do I get there?*

Soll ich hierhin oder dorthin gehen?   *Do I go here or there?*

Was kostet der Eintritt?   *How much is the entry fee?*

Gibt es Ermäßigung für Studenten?   *Is there a student reduction?*

Gibt es Ermäßigung für Kinder?   *Is there a child reduction?*

Tut man das hier?   *Does one do that here?*

Was bedeutet das?   *What does that mean?*

Was heißt das auf Deutsch?   *What's that called in German?*

Könnten Sie das bitte wiederholen?   *Could you repeat that please?*

Wie bitte?   *Pardon?*

Appendix

For your information

If you have any queries about the area you will be visiting the National Tourist Offices in London will be able to help you.

> The National German Tourist Office
> 65 Curzon Street
> London W11 7AE
> 071 495 3990

> The Swiss National Tourist Office
> The Swiss Centre
> New Coventry Street
> London W1
> 071 734 1921

> The Austrian National Tourist Office
> 30 St George Street
> London W1
> 071 629 0461

Games to play on the road

To reach your partner's home you may have to travel a long way and you might like to make up some games with your friends to relieve the monotony of motorway travelling. Here are some ideas:

European Vehicle Stickers (showing country of origin)

A	Austria	FL	Leichtenstein
AL	Albania	GB	Great Britain
AND	Andorra	GR	Greece
B	Belgium	H	Hungary
BG	Bulgaria	I	Italy
CH	Switzerland	IRL	Ireland
CS	Czechoslovakia	L	Luxembourg
D	West Germany	MC	Monaco
DDR	East Germany	N	Norway
DK	Denmark	NL	Netherlands
E	Spain	P	Portugal
F	France	PL	Poland

R	Romania	SF	Finland
RSM	San Marino	SU	Soviet Union
S	Sweden	YU	Yugoslavia
SCV	Vatican City		

a) Who can see the most different country stickers?

b) Write down all the letters seen on vehicles in one minute (or in five minutes or longer if you're not on a motorway) then choose three additional letters of the alphabet and see how many words it's possible to make. The game could be played using the letters to make English words and then afterwards to make German words.

German Vehicle Registration Plates

The letters on the number plates show the town where the car was registered. The largest cities have just their initial letter, other large towns have two letters and the smaller towns are shown by three letters, as can be seen below. There is not room here to include every registration code, so you could have fun trying to see which other ones you can spot in your travels.

A	Augsburg	K	Köln (Cologne)
B	Berlin (West)	M	München (Munich)
D	Düsseldorf	N	Nürnberg (Nuremberg)
E	Essen	S	Stuttgart
F	Frankfurt	W	Wuppertal
H	Hannover (Hanover)		

BI	Bielefeld	HM	Hameln (Hamelin)
BO	Bochum	KA	Karlsruhe
BN	Bonn	KI	Kiel
CE	Celle	KR	Krefeld
DO	Dortmund	MA	Mannheim
DU	Duisburg	MG	Mönchengladbach
ER	Erlangen	MI	Minden
FR	Freiburg	MH	Mülheim/Ruhr
GE	Gelsenkirchen	MS	Münster
GÖ	Göttingen	OB	Oberhausen
HB	(Hansestadt) Bremen	OS	Osnabruck
HH	(Hansestadt) Hamburg	TÜ	Tübingen
HL	(Hansestadt) Lübeck		

ALF	Alfeld	MES	Hochsauerland:
FAL	Fallingbostel		Meschede
		SÜW	Südlicheweinstraße

As well as seeing how many different place codes you can spot, you could make up words or try to find your initials or the initials of your friends and family.

Austrian Vehicle Registration Plates

The letter on the vehicle number plate denotes which of the nine **Länder** the car was registered in.

B	Burgenland	ST	Steiermark
K	Kärten	T	Tirol
N	Niederösterreich	V	Vorarlberg
O	Oberösterreich	W	Wien (Vienna)
S	Salzburg		

Swiss Vehicle Registration Plates

The letters on the number plate show the initial letters of the city where the car was registered. Here are some examples. How many others can you spot?

BA	Basel	GE	Geneva
BE	Bern	LU	Luzern